DERNGATE DAYS

Eileen Bebbington
née Lacey

Cover: The author aged six in her new uniform for the winter term, 1955

ISBN 0 9549 091 0 0

Published by
Eileen Bebbington
5 Pullar Avenue
Bridge of Allan
Stirling
FK9 4TB

Typeset and Printed
by Graphics & Print Services, University of Stirling

❦ Contents ❦

★ For information on forms and dates, please use the 'Details of time at school' table.

❀ Acknowledgements ❀

Over the last four years I have had to pester some people by letter more often than I would have wished because my home has been in central Scotland. I have always received kindness in return for my enquiries. I am very grateful to Michael Albert for his patience and help with my computing enquiries; to Owen Butler who was minister to the Bassett-Lowkes and who has had, and still has, a profound influence for good on my own family; and to Joan Ceybird and her daughters, Jane and Rosemary, also old girls of the school, who have gone out of their way to answer my queries. Betty Cook, Janet Dicks and her daughter, Jane Dobell, Patricia Douglas, Albert Eason (author of *St Crispin's Men*), Roy Emburey, Mary Heath, Judith Hodgkinson, Rory Kempton, Olga Meidner, Sylvia Pinches, David Walmsley, Joy Webb, Robert Webb and Carolyn White have all helped enormously. Thank you to English Heritage, to the Northampton Borough Council Museums and Heritage Services, and to the Northampton Record Society. My special thanks go to Terry Bracher, the Northamptonshire Local Studies Librarian, for his swift answers on points of detail. I want to thank Wanda Davies, once a teacher at the school, very warmly, not only for her valiant efforts to teach me to write, which, from the exercise books I still have, appears to have been an uphill struggle, but also for her encouragement in the last four years for me to persevere with this book and for her warm approval of the redevelopment of Derngate. She now lives in Albion Court on part of the old site and enthuses about where she is. I had last seen the buildings when they were derelict, a sad, sad, sight, and so it has been a real encouragement to hear her positive approach. My thanks go to my husband David for his constant interest and invaluable help with the manuscript and to my daughter Anne who has always urged me to write the book for my own pleasure, regardless of whether it ever sees the light of day. I should like my new granddaughter, Becky, to be able to find out from this book about her granny's time at school, if she would like to one day.

This little book is dedicated to my parents, Margaret Lacey and the late David Lacey, who made the original decision to send me to this school. For this I shall always be grateful.

EILEEN BEBBINGTON
Bridge of Allan
November 2004

❄ **Why this book?** ❄

Three years ago, on a visit to the newly opened Lighthouse Gallery in central Glasgow, I browsed among pictures of the work of the Scottish architect Charles Rennie Mackintosh. Many of his most famous buildings were shown there: Hill House, Glasgow School of Art and so on. Tucked among them was a photograph of 78 Derngate. The 'Derngate' was in large letters; underneath was 'Northampton' in small ones. I realised that not many people in that room would know much about Northampton, never mind Derngate. Almost certainly no one else had spent fourteen formative years of their life in and around that short road as I had done from 1953 to 1966 as a pupil of Northampton High School for Girls. Just as the world of the Bassett-Lowkes who commissioned Mackintosh to redesign their house has now disappeared, so has the era of hundreds of schoolgirls dotting in and out among the Derngate houses, because in 1992 the school moved to spanking new buildings at Hardingstone, a village just south of the town. My time came at the end of the Bassett-Lowke era. The two worlds come together because in 1964 the school bought Mackintosh House, becoming custodians of the house and acquiring listed Grade 2 status for it. Later in the 1970s it was used as yet another space for pupils, this time sixth formers, until it became, along with Becket House, one of the most important historic buildings in the town today.

Derngate was a magical place to be at school. Behind the constant traffic and, in those days, all the United Counties buses hurrying home to their terminus (where the Derngate Centre now is), lay wonderful gardens and green areas. An elegant mixture of Georgian and Victorian buildings spread over the site, blended with modern twentieth-century ones. Inconvenient? Yes. Wet and cold at times? Certainly. But the beauty of that site deeply influenced us. In this short book I have drawn on my school reports, speech day programmes, newspaper cuttings, photographs and quite detailed diaries that I kept at the time, as well as two books, *The First Hundred Years* and *44 Derngate*, which cover the history of the life of the school until it moved to Hardingstone. My hope is that I can share some of the magic as I record my experiences of 'Derngate Days'.

❀ So where is Northampton? ❀

Northampton, a county town right in the middle of England, lies almost as far away from the coast as it is possible to be, a constant sadness for my parents who had moved up from Bournemouth in 1946. In the middle ages, Northampton had been a flourishing medieval centre with a castle, located close to the site of the modern railway station. In 1164 Thomas Becket, Archbishop of Canterbury, had been tried and condemned to death in this castle before making a dramatic escape. Derngate itself had connections with Becket since Becket's Well is just beyond it and Becket's Park across the road. In 1215 Northampton became the focus of civil unrest under King John. The town had long been famous for boot and shoe making; I have clear memories of visits from school to the Guildhall Museum to draw medieval shoes. In the 1950s and 60s, when I lived there, the population was around 100,000. In the 1970s a huge expansion took place with new areas springing up to house London overspill and by 1981 numbers reached 145,000. All sorts of rumours spread; at one stage it was said that Northampton should be developed as far as Wellingborough. The town did not become that big, but it did grow a great deal bigger after I left.

❀ And Derngate? ❀

Derngate is one of the roads leading south-east from the town centre. In medieval times there had been a gate about half way down it, and a watchtower, possibly part of the old town walls, had stood near the site of number 66. From old maps we can see that by 1847 the road had been developed with houses, and the bottom end was known as Waterloo Terrace until 1938. We may think of traffic noise as a modern phenomenon, but in 1922 school inspectors complained that the school could be very noisy from the horses and carts as they passed by on the cobbles. Pollution certainly increased once the impressive United Counties Bus Station opened in 1935. We are concerned in this book with the houses developed on the south side of the road in a triangle that is also bordered by Albion Place and Victoria Promenade.

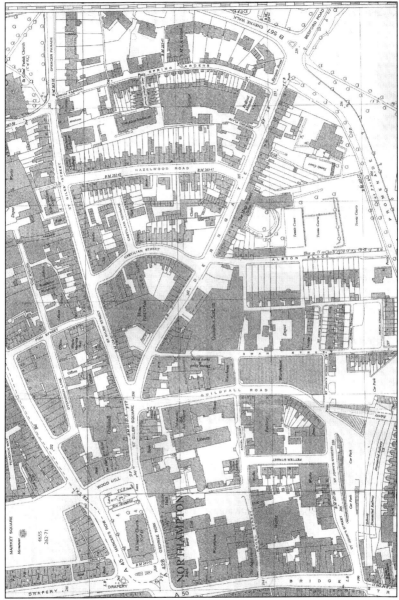

A 1964 map of the south-east sector of the town, showing the extent of the High School buildings and grounds towards the bottom right. The town centre with Mercer's Row and the market square is at the top left.

Reproduced by permission of Ordnance Survey on behalf of The Controller of Her Majesty's Stationery Office, © Crown Copyright 100043320

❀ First visit to Derngate ❀

The first and only interview in my life at a new school took place in very early 1953 when I was four and a half. My mother and I travelled from home in Abington Avenue on the number eight bus down to Towerfield (66 Derngate) to see if I was a suitable new pupil. (The building must have been where the junior department of the High School for Girls was run. I would not be a pupil in it for another four years). That was the only time I ever remember going through the big front door. The whole building seemed very dark and brown as we sat in the hall to wait while our shoes squeaked on the highly polished wooden floor. Then we were asked into the room off the hall which overlooked the garden. I do not remember who interviewed me; I can clearly remember being asked to close the door and to say what some rather grubby colours were in a bunch of small pieces of woven material. I must have passed these challenges because three months later I became a pupil of Northampton High School for Girls at its junior department in Springhill in Cliftonville, off the Billing Road.

❀ The story of the High School ❀

The school was started in 1878 in Abington Street in the so-called Clevedon buildings under the auspices of the local Church of England school managers. Called firstly 'The Northampton Middle-Class Girls School', it was subsequently known as 'The Clevedon School, a Church High School'. By 1885 it had become one of the Church School Company schools; the Company, like the Girls' Public Day School Trust, had come into being to manage many of the new middle-class girls' schools which had sprung up in the second half of the nineteenth century. The premises at 83 Abington Street, near the corner of Lower Mounts, rapidly became too small despite a donation of £1000 from the owner, a Mr Phipps, and so the institution moved to Castilian House in Castilian Street in 1914 and from there to 44 Derngate in 1921. The school went through some difficult years at the end of the century and again in the 1920s. Competition was fierce, with as many as fourteen other girls' schools in the town in 1892.

The school, greatly helped by the 1902 Education Act which turned it into a Direct Grant institution, began to receive a number of scholars from both town and county and so became assured of a regular income. I was therefore a pupil around roughly the middle of the school's history. I had definite links with the early years; Miss Phipps, who took me in IPH, was the daughter of the first owner of the Abington Street buildings. She seemed quite old to us and had joined the staff in 1925, but continued teaching until her retirement in 1965. Again, when I was in the sixth form, I was asked to visit Miss Gibbins, who had become a pupil in 1890 aged seven, and who had then taught at the school, becoming Deputy Head before retiring in 1946. Finally, I was there for over two years of Miss Lightburne's reign which was to go on until her retirement in 1988, and so my links cover a span of some one hundred years.

❀ Derngate visits from Springhill ❀

It is easy to remember when I started at Springhill, the junior department of the school, set in the wonderfully leafy road called Cliftonville, which ran off Billing Road just above the General Hospital. Starting in April 1953 when the flowers were on the huge horse chestnut trees, I went into the class of the wonderful Miss Cook, the perfect first teacher. I did not know at the time but Springhill had been the childhood home of Miss Ince-Jones who taught music and who played rousing marches, like Schubert's *Marche Militaire*, to accompany us marching out of prayers in the morning. Her father had run a progressive school for deaf children in their house. The wonderful garden was not taking kindly to having a tarmac play area imposed on what had been the vegetable patch. Each year the rhubarb still managed to push its way up! In the June that term for the coronation of Queen Elizabeth, I received my celebratory mug as well as a slim black New Testament from the school; I remember visiting friends who had a tiny black and white television set on which to watch the event. I do not think I was very interested in the ceremony, but I do remember extra playing time.

Our visits to the main building in Derngate, although not frequent, were memorable. Each July we would have our Sports Day on the bottom grass pitch which seemed huge to my eyes, alongside Victoria Promenade. There we jumped about in sacks, tried to keep porcelain eggs on spoons as we raced along, ran three-legged races tied at the ankle to a friend, skipped and collected bean bags. My speciality was the treacle tin race! I was adept at walking along on two Tate and Lyle – empty – treacle tins with a loop of twine threaded through them to hold, no easy matter on the lumpy bumpy surface. Sadly this aptitude did not transfer into other athletic skills. The parents sat on the hard wooden chairs brought down from the main school and cheered our efforts. Once we reached Towerfield (aged 9) there were no more Sports Days.

We also visited the Main School just before each Christmas for the Toy Service, always conducted by the Bishop of Peterborough. This awe-inspiring occasion when the whole school, maybe 7-800 girls with a few boys under eight, crowded into the Hall, clutching toys they had been persuaded to surrender for children less fortunate than themselves, never ceased to move me. We did not always give up our toys willingly; it was stressed they had to be in excellent condition so that we could not offload a broken doll which was not needed any more! I enjoyed the carols; I feel we had a very impressive range of them, starting from 'The Little Fir Tree', which I loved, to 'Three Kings from Persian Lands Afar', which was virtually unknown at that time. Mr Tudor, a singing master, travelled regularly to the school from the Westminster Abbey choir. We probably owed these carols to him.

Last year at Springhill. Form IIc in part of the beautiful garden.

The most memorable visit was the Foundation Stone Laying Ceremony of the new Hall and Gym block in 1954. Having walked down to Derngate in the pouring rain, we had to leave our panama hats and blazers on desks at the very top of Towerfield (which seemed nearly in the sky!). Then we went to stand for a very, very long time in the pouring rain on the main school hard court, just in our thin, short-sleeved summer frocks. (On any special occasion the weather was not allowed to be a factor. If summer frocks had been decreed, then frocks it was!) I only vaguely remember the ceremony itself but eventually we traipsed damply back to the top of Towerfield only to find that our panama hats had been soaking up ink from the open inkwells into their damp material and were ruined. My mother was not amused. Nor was she pleased to have me at home for the next two weeks with a bad cold. I fared better than the Countess Spencer who had come from Althorp to lay the foundation stone. Apparently she slipped on the wet grass before she left and badly sprained her ankle. I knew nothing of this as I was more concerned about soggy pale blue panama and its consequences!

✵ Links with the Spencers ✵

We always regarded the Spencers as one of our 'local families' who would come to give out prizes or open a building for us. Indeed the Countess Spencer of 1887 had been one of the original patrons. The Countess who laid the stone in the wet was the grandmother of the late Princess of Wales. It was a shock in 1997 when suddenly Althorp became the centre of world media attention as Princess Diana's burial was beamed across the globe. Television commentators started to say things like 'far away in the depths of rural Northamptonshire'; I felt quite incensed. After all, the M1 motorway was only a stone's throw away.

We had other links with the Spencers. A few of us from school used to ride at the stables attached to East Haddon Hall School; from there we would hack down on our ponies across the main road and up to Great Brington, the Althorp estate village. This intrigued me as the thatched cottages were still numbered in one sequence: they were also in dire need of repair. If we had time we rode through the Althorp estate and home.

Lady Diana's two older sisters, Lady Sarah and Lady Jane Spencer, boarded at the school and kept their ponies there so we saw them frequently on Saturdays in term time.

The Spencers were only one of our local historic families. In 1952 HRH The Duchess of Gloucester had laid the foundation stone for the new Science Block. She lived at Barnwell: although this was at the other end of our very long county she was still regarded as a 'local'. The county was full of titled families and many had children in the Pytchley Pony Club. Often we would hack home with the Honourable James Lowther, the future owner of Holdenby House. The High School itself was sometimes used by these families as a prep school. Both Lady Eliza and Lady Judith Compton, daughters of the Marquis of Northampton, attended Springhill at this time before going on elsewhere. We felt quite important to have the Manningham-Buller sisters at the school for a while because their father, later Lord Dilhorne, was obviously something important in London (I think he was the Attorney General at that time) though we did not have a clue what he did. (Maybe we really did live in the depths of nowhere!) Eliza, or Elizabeth as she was then known, moved on elsewhere; at present she heads MI5.

I experienced feudal England at first hand when the Religious Knowledge teacher in UV took us to visit Easton Neston, a large country house near Towcester which local people considered a main contender for being the location of Jane Austen's Mansfield Park. At that time it was not open to the public and so this was quite exciting. The teacher was a tenant of Lady Hesketh, whose husband's family had owned the estate for centuries. While she showed us round the house, we were very intrigued to see our teacher tugging his forelock and saying 'Yes my lady' and 'No my lady' and asking after Master John, the future Lord Hesketh of motor racing fame, then aged twelve and away at school.

❀ A Towerfield pupil ❀

After four years and one term at the light and airy Springhill house, it was quite a shock to become a pupil at Towerfield, 66 Derngate. Now we could not use the front door but went in through a small door on the right of the building; this led into a small cloakroom with pegs and shoebags (old black-out material from the Second World War with each girl's name embroidered in gold!). From there we went through an open doorway into the old house itself. If we wanted to go downstairs at break time, we would go down the narrow twisting staircase to a garden room where the 1d (0.4p) currant buns were sold, together with the one third of a pint of milk which was provided for us by the government as part of post-war nutrition. Often the bottles, warm from being outside in the sun, had already been pecked opened by blue-tits on the doorstep. To go upstairs to our classroom we would turn round into the dark, gloomy hall and up the dark brown stairs into the room on the right. Running the whole depth of the building, this room was unusual in being higher at the back

The author as a Towerfield pupil, 1958. Note the short white socks, the white gloves and the turned-up winter hat.

than the front. Since the teacher sat below us, we could have a good look from the back desks out on to the activities of Derngate undetected.

In Towerfield we started to use a system of monitresses for just about all the jobs that could be conceived. Door monitresses jumped to open and shut the door for visitors to a form room (the whole form had to leap to its feet if an adult entered and reply loudly in unison if spoken to). If on ink duty, the monitress had to take round an enormous bottle of evil-smelling, non-washable dark blue ink to fill up the open inkwells at each desk. My memory of these is that they were usually plugged by pieces of blotting paper that bored girls had torn up. At the start of each term, we were supplied, through the stationery monitress, a much coveted post, with all our colour-coded exercise books, a wooden pen-holder (with a separate nib, always italic), a rubber, a ruler and a sheet of very bright pink blotting paper. Only once we reached the Main School could we use Osmiroid fountain pens, with italic nibs still, of course. I am not sure why pens all had to be italic. They were not easy to use in the younger years. Usually by the end of the day, at least three fingers would be stained deep blue, as well as parts of my summer dress, and the nib would have become

A 1980s view of the south side of Towerfield, with number 68 on its right, looking towards Becket House.

crossed. Biros were almost unknown and certainly not to be used. If we wanted colour, we took up our Lakeland crayons.

Contact with the Main School now increased; Miss Marsden, the Main School headmistress herself, appeared once a week to take a mental arithmetic lesson in the smaller teaching room running across the back of the building. A terrifying experience! Each lesson started with a Ten Test with the questions fired off at great speed and she spent a lot of time teaching us short cuts. To this day I am a wizard divider – or is it multiplier – of 25s. But sadly I had very little understanding of maths in general and became totally confused. My mother became quite angry that we were learning short cuts BEFORE learning the basics! Discipline in those lessons was strict with a red-haired older girl called Karen patrolling the rows of desks with a ruler. She never used it on a pupil but hearing her whacking it on the desk was enough to quell any thought of a whisper to one's neighbour. This strict atmosphere came as a shock after the more relaxed atmosphere at the end of our time in Spring Hill. There Miss Beesley, the head, had ruled with a firm hand, but within our form the atmosphere had been lively. Occasionally one's mother might be 'sent for', which meant a girl would be in real trouble when she reached home. I was once pulled out of line in Prayers for talking and then talked again as the others left. I was in serious hot water when the school complained to my parents.

From Towerfield we visited the Main School for some activities such as gym and the end-of-term "Prayers". We also, I find from old exam papers, now had these tests twice a year. In the 1959 geography paper I see we were asked to write a paragraph on the Kirghiz. I hope I knew more about that/them than I do now!

❀ Towerfield Garden ❀

However dark the inside of the Towerfield house may have been, its glory was the garden. Apart from the hard court that had been fitted in, it could easily be imagined that the last Edwardian family of the house had only just moved out, leaving the garden for a while. The downstairs room where we drank our warm milk had a garden door opening on to a small gravel area which led directly to a narrow lawn. The long, thin gardens of the whole row of houses, including 78, stretched from the back of the Derngate buildings right down to Victoria Promenade. To the right, fat goldfish swam lazily around a sizeable pond, waiting for pieces of our currant buns. (What would the health and safety experts make of this pond now? Yet I cannot remember one of us falling in, never mind drowning in it.

As with the whole High School site, there was a big drop between the levels of front and back, and so the netball/tennis court, squeezed in really tightly, lay considerably below the lawn. Other schools coming to play matches could find the restricted space at the side very off-putting. A doubles tennis match was a real challenge! Below the court, on a lower level again, stood the semi-disused greenhouse where Albert, the ancient gardener, pottered; below there were the remains of an extensive vegetable garden. By this time only a few asparagus plants and salad vegetables with some flowers for decoration grew there, but it all seemed very much as it had been left. Down the whole of the right side of the garden ran a gravel path next to an old brick boundary wall on which grew wonderful ancient rambling roses with ivy and creeper spreading along it. My favourite season has always been autumn; the hips, haws and ivy flowers all along this wall gave a feeling of ancient roots and reassuring continuity.

❈ 68 Derngate ❈

For the second year in Towerfield we spent most of our day in 68 Derngate which the school had only recently bought. Our classroom ran the whole depth of the house; once again one end presented a good view of Derngate life with the teacher seemingly miles away at the other. We still used the old Towerfield cloakroom, just running out of 68 into 66.

Miss Thornton presided over our form, LIIIT. She took us for nearly everything; in her class I had a stand-off for about half a term in sewing because I could not thread my needle and she would not thread it for me! I think by then we were making a skirt out of checked gingham material. (Everything in sewing was made of gingham - I still have a handkerchief case and a stocking container sewn on to a coat hanger which my mother kept for the next forty years!) Because of the needle - threading controversy I never finished my skirt and by then had outgrown it anyway! That was the end of my sewing career. Mercifully my daughter never needed her name embroidered on to a shoe bag.

Miss Thornton, one of the first people from further north that I had met, told us many tales of Sheffield and the industry there. It seemed like a far-away world. The M1 was only just opening, giving easier access to areas we would not otherwise have visited. We felt very proud in 1959 to have the very first motorway link to London so near to home. I had seen it built inch by inch as my father, a civil engineer with Kottler and Heron, based in Cliftonville, Northampton, took us on Sunday afternoon walks to view progress. We were so excited by the new motorway service areas that we would go for a treat to the Newport Pagnell one or, later, if we were ambitious, to Leicester Forest East! It seemed amazing to eat a meal while traffic roared underneath.

It was during my time in this class that one of our fellow pupils was killed. All through the school we had a free half-day each week; on one morning after a half day we were told that Linda Watson had been taking her pony, Toffee, to the blacksmith when the pony shied at a bus; Linda was thrown and killed. In a sombre atmosphere, Miss Thornton told us later all about the funeral. I am afraid that the overriding concern for many of us was what was to happen to Toffee. None of us could bear to think of him being put down.

This was the year when a few of us took the Eleven-Plus exam. We could have continued at the school anyway if our parents had been willing to pay fees, but my parents, unsure about a job move for my father, wanted me to take the exam anyway. I had some extra coaching outside school, since there was no preparation in school, with endless practice of the 'If eight men dig a ditch in three days, how many days would it take twelve and a half men' variety! Just a few of us went up to the Notre Dame Convent School then in Abington Street to sit the exam. I was fortunate and passed, and so the local education authority paid my fees.

❀ The Main School, 44 Derngate: the original building ❀

At the age of eleven, those of us who were continuing into the Main School made the short move along Derngate to its very impressive buildings. No strangers to some of them, we now explored their full range. The core of the main school consisted of a large Georgian house, 44 Derngate, which had been the vicarage of All Saints' Church in the middle of the town. The last vicar to have lived there sounds to have been a rather jolly man who held garden parties every summer with a bandstand where the tennis courts were later to be. If we went in by the front door, again out of bounds to us and looked after for an amazing number of years by an ageless lady called Millie, we entered a cool, stone-flagged large hall. On the right was the small medical room where offenders were sent each first day of term if their mothers had forgotten to send back the medical certificate. Three or four classrooms opened off this hall including room 3 overlooking the garden on the left. In summer afternoons the desire to doze off as tennis rackets gently pinged outside was very nearly irresistible. A very elegant Scottish teacher of English, called Miss Euphemia Sinton, seemed to use this room a lot; I can remember struggling to stay awake for her pleasant voice as the sound of tennis rackets wafted gently through the huge windows. Again in this room a chemistry teacher knitted on metal needles all the way through our exam which she was invigilating.

Two staircases led up to the first floor, the left strictly for up traffic and the right one for down. On the landing at the front were two small staffrooms with at the back two large classrooms possessing glorious views down across the gardens to Becket's Park. Between them lay the headmistress's study so if one was 'sent for', one had to stand in full view of the

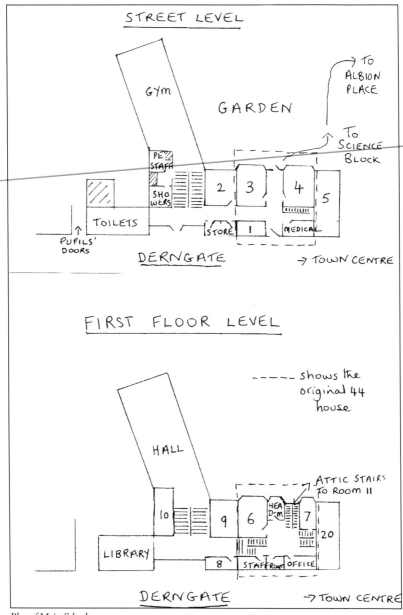

STREET LEVEL

GYM

GARDEN

→ TO ALBION PLACE

→ To SCIENCE BLOCK

PE STAFF

SHO WERS

2   3   4   5

TOILETS

STORE   1   MEDICAL

↑ PUPILS' DOORS

DERNGATE

→ TOWN CENTRE

FIRST FLOOR LEVEL

------ shows the original 44 house

HALL

ATTIC STAIRS TO ROOM 11

10   9   6   HEA D-m   7   20

LIBRARY

8   STAFFROOM   OFFICE

DERNGATE

→ TOWN CENTRE

Plan of Main School

staff room. Up off the landing twisted and climbed a very narrow staircase up to three much used attics; one of them became my first form room where I went each morning. Having negotiated the stairs - no chance of one-way traffic here - we had to duck down under the roof beams to get to our tables. Our books and pens were kept in lockers the other side of the roof beams. This room was lit by a small window, through which a few intrepid older pupils used to climb out on to the roof of 42 Derngate, which had been bought in 1955, to sunbathe. Never mind fishponds! What with the stairs and the roof access, this really was dangerous living, but we accepted it as perfectly normal.

Two large rooms to the right side of 44 stretched the depth of the building, one for geography and one at first for art and later for various subjects. Number 42 provided an extension to 44; access was through the garden. Painted in simple white throughout, the house seemed characterless. The old vicarage itself had a splendid white south door into the garden through which we were eventually allowed to go as sixth formers. This was where a large hand bell was rung at every change of lesson.

Along to the right from the front door, a twisting stone staircase led down to the basement. This must surely have required one-way traffic! Down here in a narrow rabbit warren of passages, the dining room (room 14) was to be found. The whole of this basement area always smelled of cooking and was hot and stuffy. I had a difficult year at school in UIVJ when our form room consisted of this old room, well below ground level, with its trestle tables, backless benches and old cupboards for storing our books. I wonder now if these surroundings had anything to do with how I felt? Also downstairs lay some very crowded and stuffy cloakrooms with more embroidered shoe bags and on a wet day an almost suffocating smell of drying gaberdine. The whole of number 44 felt like someone's private house in which we were visitors.

✿ The Main School: the new building ✿

I was very fortunate to be at the school in this period because the new buildings had opened only in 1957, one year before we started to use some of them from Towerfield; they certainly provided a spacious and attractive

A 1970s view of the back of 44 Derngate. In the 1950s, shrubs grew in front of the downstairs classroom windows.

environment for us and it was a shock to hear that they had been demolished for the redevelopment as 'old' structures'! They, and many other buildings yet to come, had been largely funded by members of the Cripps family. First Sir Cyril and later Sir Humphrey, who died only in 2000, donated many thousands of pounds to the school as well as to institutions like the General Hospital and Nottingham University. Their Pianoforte Supplies Company factory lay next to the main railway line in the village of Roade; we never quite understood what the Supplies meant or how they could be so profitable! The family had several connections with the school, Sir Humphrey's sister being my form teacher in 1953-1954. He himself later became chair of the Governors and was instrumental in the move to the new site at Hardingstone.

I had never been in buildings of this scale before. Some of the old Derngate properties had disappeared to make the new possible. The school had purchased Eagle House (number 46), and later demolished it together with two other houses. 44 was then connected across the gap with a red brick building, in which large blue double gates led down a sharp slope into the site itself. At right angles to Derngate, a huge (as it seemed to me) building which contained the Hall and the Gym extended right down to the halfway point of the whole site. This had replaced an old tin hut that had been there for many years in which Prayers had been held and plays performed. It was always spoken of with affection by those who remembered it.

Under street level lay new cloakrooms - definitely less smelly than the old ones. Up a few steps and we reached an open mezzanine outside the Gym and the changing rooms; through double doors and we were looking down on the Gym, seemingly miles below us. Because the whole site is on a steep hill, the different sections had to be terraced. We could go down by stairs right or left into the Gym - a very cold space on a winter's morning either for gym or public exams. All the equipment we could think of could be found in the Gym, and the games staff could look down

The Hall and Gymnasium building.

on us from the window in their staff room, high up in the wall. On one occasion a student teacher, Miss Tilley, trapped her finger under the weight of one huge section of wall bars so someone had to be despatched at high speed up the steps to fetch help. I remember her ashen face and grim determination to be brave to this day.

If we turned back and climbed more stairs from the mezzanine level, we were on street level with a smart front door used on Speech Days and play performances. To the right and through swing doors lay a set of toilets with all the doors painted a strange pinky orange colour, the largest set of toilets I supposed I had ever seen. (This was probably quite true. Only motorway services would have more and the M1 did not open until 1959.) There were plenty of toilets, but I never felt at ease in such a large area. Straight on from the toilets would lead to the old door of 44 but up more stairs again to the left, we would be in another open area outside the Hall.

No expense had been spared on the new building. A great deal of neutrally coloured marble made these open areas calming and cool. The huge Hall straight ahead had long grey curtains and grey canvas-and-metal chairs. At the far end was a fully equipped stage complete with lighting, together, underneath, with the dressing rooms and the costume store. We had no idea how fortunate we were to have all these facilities. A smallish curtained room led off the back of the Hall (room 10), a noisy setting for a classroom. In this form room in VI 1, I came to know Caroline Bradley who was later to become an international show jumper and, sadly, to die at a young age. Going back up some more stairs, we would now be above street level in an open area used for displays such as cake icing from O Level cookery candidates. To the right lay the new light, airy Library, while to the left the explorer could pass two class rooms and join up with the 44 house again, just below staff room level. Sad though it was that Eagle House was demolished, the architects had used its site brilliantly, giving us a great deal of open space to develop in.

❀ The Main School Garden ❀

As with Towerfield, the glory of the Main School was the garden. Huge copper beech trees overhung us as we played. A large lawn (Thou shalt not walk on that!) surrounded by formal flower beds lay immediately outside the south door of number 44; then there was a drop down to a wonderful herbaceous border with lupins and delphiniums in summer and on to the hard court; down a short bank again we reached three grass tennis courts side by side (Thou shalt not walk on those either!). Down a really steep bank beyond that we came to the huge grass area alongside Victoria Promenade with plenty of space for several more tennis courts and rounders pitches. Both sides of the garden contained enough spare space to let us walk down past the tennis courts to reach the Art Block or the bottom grass. Very few girls' day schools at this time had nine or ten tennis courts on site. With the majority of grass courts, we were very dependent on the weather, but when we had other school teams to visit, it meant we could play many matches simultaneously.

The Main School garden as it was in the 1950s. Victoria Promenade runs along the wall at the bottom.

❀ The Science Block ❀

Down the Albion Place side of the garden stood the Science Block which had opened in 1954: on the left of it upstairs a well-equipped biology laboratory, downstairs two classrooms with a folding wooden partition between them. This big room was a good idea in principle - on wet days prayers could be held here to save us drowning on the way to the hall - but the temperamental partition often did not quite close and so it was always possible to hear everything on the other side of it. A noisy class one side interrupted the other. On the right upstairs of the block lay the chemistry room, a light space with beautiful bright blue crystals growing in solutions. Downstairs was the rather bleak physics lab, always dark with overhanging trees.

❈ The Cripps Block ❈

In 1958 a new block, again funded by Cripps money, appeared down at the bottom of the Derngate gardens with a gate on to Victoria Promenade. This contained a large dining hall, an art room and a domestic science room complete with the latest gas and electric cookers. I never had warm feelings towards this block. The DS room for example, below ground level, always seemed dark. Another of the wonderful copper beech trees overhung the whole building. The art room provided a splendid view into Becket's Park which helped while away the time since I did not enjoy the art we did. (I usually managed to arrange my extra speech lessons in art periods!) I never used the dining room.

❈ Becket House ❈

The school policy at this time of continuing to buy houses along Derngate meant that in 1962 Becket House, number 82, became school property. It stood at the far end of the road, overlooking Becket's Park. As with number 42, it had been painted plain white throughout, which gave it a rather forlorn feel. Used at first for music and speech lessons, this policy had to be changed later because of noise problems. I remember that in speech lessons on the top floor of Becket House, the chairs always felt as though they were sliding towards the window! When I stood up opposite the window to say my poem, I felt I could have ski-ed smoothly across the polished floor right into the huge trees in the garden. I believe that soon afterwards the building was found to be unsafe and urgent structural work had to be done. This garden, not accessible to us, had the tallest, most wonderful trees in it. All the gardens to the right of Becket House, 78 included, contained remarkable trees and shrubs. A huge monkey-puzzle seemed very exotic; that was certainly not typical of Northampton flora. As we walked along to Becket House, we would pass 78 and see the tiny panes of glass always dirty from the traffic fumes. I always felt sorry for anyone who had to clean them.

View across the Towerfield hard court towards Mackintosh House and Becket House. The whole area was a mass of shrubs and trees.

❀ 58 Derngate ❀

Another house bought during my time, number 58, once again was used for small group teaching. The position of this house, directly opposite a large veterinary practice called Sutton and Cook's, caused some real problems. At three p.m. on the same day each week, an open lorry called to collect the bodies of all the dogs that had been put down recently. At that point our excellent sixth form history teacher, Miss Dimmock, on the first floor of number 58 was trying to get to grips with the English Civil War. You can imagine the screams and hysteria that broke out each week as the lorry pulled out of the yard opposite. The bodies, hidden from pedestrians, lay in full view of our upstairs window!

6 and 7 Albion Place. Note the gardens at the front.

❀ 6 and 7 Albion Place ❀

Albion Place, on the town side of the site, consisted of more elegant early Victorian town houses. Miss Marsden, headmistress at the time, had wanted the school to expand down that stretch as well. In 1946 the governors purchased number 7, but a year or so later they could not afford to buy number 6 and so Miss Marsden bought it herself and rented it to the school. Most of the rooms were staff bedsits and the staff dining room, but a teaching room in 7 on the first floor and the third-year sixth girls' common room provided extra, much needed space. (The usual time to apply to Oxbridge then was the term after A Levels. Pupils then often had a gap of six months, rather than a year.) The gardens of these houses lay at the front and had a cottage garden feel which spoke of a previous era. A really beautiful building called Corinth House had stood below the Albion Place terrace of houses, but that was demolished in the 1960s to make a Corporation car park. I remember even then being sad. Today it would be a listed building and possibly safe. Built in 1845, it had been the Royal Victoria Dispensary, built to mark Queen Victoria passing through the town. Again I later read that Miss Marsden had tried to buy that when new premises were needed for the younger classes, but the school could not afford it and waited to buy Towerfield. I might easily have been a pupil of Corinth House!

❦ School uniform ❦

So what did all these schoolgirls look like as they dotted in and out of the Derngate houses? Fashion gurus today claim that black and navy should never be worn together, but the combination seems normal to me as the school uniform combined the two. In Springhill we wore navy pleated skirts with two straps over the shoulder, but then graduated to a navy pinafore dress or skirt with a white shirt and – note – a black and golden-yellow tie; a navy cardigan or V-necked jumper optional; grey socks in the junior years (hand me downs from my brother) then white ankle socks and eventually and daringly, beige stockings or tights! In Springhill and Towerfield we had wonderful winter coats as shown on the cover of this book, but later had to make do with navy gaberdine raincoats. Until the second-year sixth we had to wear a black velour hat with a yellow and gold hatband in winter and a pale panama hat with hatband in summer. The black hats at the start turned up, as in the cover photo, but I still have my later one which turned down; I did not like this one because it always rubbed on the back of our collars. All through the year we could wear the black school blazer with a large gold school badge on the pocket. In the summer in the pocket would have to be white gloves! Normally most of us would wear the gloves anyway, but on school trips or the Ascension Day walk through the town to All Saints Church, gloves were regarded as essential; no one could set off until spare ones had been found for offenders who had forgotten. My white gloves always seemed grubby at best and absolutely filthy at worst. A black and gold striped woolly scarf could be worn in winter with a different one for the sixth form, more like a college scarf.

Then there were the summer dresses! I loved the junior ones of red, yellow or green checked gingham with short sleeves. But in the Main School we had to have dresses ordered from London, another matter altogether. Made from yellow and white striped stiffish material, the collar and reveres looked smart but they were tight in at the waist and could stick out. As a well-built adolescent I was made to feel unattractive and they proved amazingly hard to iron! (We had little to complain about over uniform. My mother at school in Bournemouth in the 1920s had to play cricket in the summer against local boys' prep schools wearing white shantung knee-length dresses with thick black woollen stockings!)

Come rain or shine, high days and holidays, we had to wear a shoulder purse for our bus fares or pass. A friend reminded me that on Speech Day this had to be taken off and worn UNDER the shirt and tie or dress which could lead to chaos on the buses going home! Most of the uniform came at first from Carne's outfitters in Abington Street and later from Saundersons on the Kettering Road. We had to make special visits since our buses went down the Wellingborough Road. I developed a very large head very young; on every visit we made to Carne's I always surprised the gentlemen serving about how big my head was!

I loved school uniform, especially in winter; I felt safe and comfortable in it. Once we could wear our own clothes in the final term of the second year and in the third-year sixth, I became much more uncomfortable. We could not buy affordable separates such as Top Shop and Logo sell these days. Clothes were much more of an investment; we would just have one or two jumpers and skirts and a Sunday dress apart from riding clothes, which cost a great deal and had to be birthday and Christmas presents.

Summer uniform in the Upper Vth, complete with shoulder purse and white gloves.

The summer dresses always seemed to stick out. Notice the stockings with seams.

Winter uniform on first passport photo, 1962.

The photographer for the Repertory Theatre, Bryan Douglas, used to play hockey with my father. In 1965 I had a sequence of photos taken in dramatic pose!

❀ Games ❀

Not surprisingly with extensive grounds at our disposal, Games loomed large in our school day; my 1962 and 1963 diaries give details of each Games lesson, which teachers took us and so on. We followed a basic rhythm of netball and hockey in the winter, tennis and swimming in the summer, with gym all the year round and dance in the early main school years. No athletics or badminton featured on the timetable. In LIVL I see we did dancing and double hockey on the same day which I considered 'heavenly' at the time! Although there was room for a hockey pitch on the bottom grass, I never remember playing there – maybe because that turned into tennis courts each summer. We either played down in Becket's Park across Victoria Promenade or we would go up to the Racecourse. This required a walk up through the Arcade to catch a bus in Abington Street to take us up Kettering Road. The changing rooms at the Racecourse seemed left from a bygone era – the last racing had been in 1904 - and it could be extremely bleak. In Becket's Park I actually caused the school a lot of expense in lost hockey balls! Keen as I was on hockey at this stage, I played on the right wing – the river side. Miss Williams used to whack the ball across to me and I, as a lightning runner, should have stopped it!

Usually I did not and another lost hockey ball would go floating away down the Nene towards the Wash! In my most energetic years I sometimes cycled from my home in the suburb of Weston Favell to Derngate in the morning, then to the Racecourse from school and finally home again, a distance of nearly five quite hilly miles! Amazing! I loved the hockey uniform, another special order; thick grey V-necked pullover, white aertex blouse, thick grey divided skirt and black canvas hockey boots. The hockey sticks were long, very unlike the short stubby ones of today.

I also greatly enjoyed netball, played on the two hard courts in grey shorts and white shirt with black plimsolls on our feet. 'Trainers' belonged very much to the future. In around Upper IV Dunlop Green Flash white canvas tennis shoes became popular. Their whiteness gleamed, at least when they had been cleaned with liquid whitener, compared with our all-black diet of shoes before this. In the summer we had fairly relaxed tennis lessons on all our courts (the teachers could not check on all of us all of the time!). For the members of the tennis teams, coaching after school became a more serious business. The first tennis six, much respected, did outstandingly well nationally; I occasionally played for the third Under 15 team and often we lost matches to Kettering or Wellingborough High by 150 games to 3 or something similar! Every Monday morning the match results were read out in Prayers. We always hoped that the first six had won a spectacular victory to cover up our own results! Mr Blincow of the Spinney Hill Tennis Club came weekly to coach us, but I had to choose between Greek and tennis in LV and Greek won.

Swimming was fun because it entailed an optionally leisurely stroll up Hazelwood Road through the Cooperative Arcade to Abington Street, and a cut-through from Lady's Lane which came out opposite the Mounts Baths. Keen swimmers could run. Others of us did not, and there was an excellent tiny sweet shop on the corner that sold wonderful sherbert dabs and liquorice. We had to get to hockey on time because the game could not start without us, but stragglers reaching the swimming pool could go undetected. The Mounts was an impressive pool with a full set of diving boards, a rare luxury half a century later. Every summer term we would have swimming sports with form teams competing and yours truly diving in for the once and only time in her life at the start of a race! Every year we watched in amazement as the three Brown sisters, Susan, Jill and Wendy (who was in our class so we felt reflected glory), swooped and somersaulted gracefully from breathtaking heights. I never got past the springboard personally! I am told that the staff dressed up and jumped into the pool at the end of the sports, but my memory of that is hazy.

Older girls dancing on the lawn in the early sixties. I am glad I have no photo of our version of Robin Hood!

Which leaves gym and dance. Gym was tolerable in parts; I never actually managed to climb even six inches up a rope, but I enjoyed Shipwreck at the end of each term when we had to escape being caught without putting a foot on the ground. There had been a long interest in gymnastics and later Swedish Drill in the school. In the 1890s large inter-schools competitions were held, but in my time there were no competitions or awards, unlike the ASA swimming awards. It was the showers and the gym dresses that were horrendous. I do not think I had ever used showers before; several of us resorted to desperate measures to escape them. I still avoid them if I can. I think the gym dresses may have been a relic from the 1920s when Greek Dancing was a common part of the curriculum of respectable girls' schools. Mine was a strange greeny blue colour made of an extremely crushable linen-type material, straight up and down to mid-thigh with a belt round the waist and, worst of all, sleeveless. They also had enormous matching knickers. To this day I will not wear anything sleeveless! They were also pretty chilly to wear, especially in the Gym in the early morning.

Dance was taken by Miss Rowlands, a retired ballet dancer, no doubt very artistic but rather strange in my eyes. Apparently when King George VI died in 1952, she led a slow pavane all round the school including up and down the attic stairs. I can well imagine it! My most vivid memory was of a presentation on the Main School lawn where we had to dance the story of Robin Hood. I was a rather plump Friar Tuck who had considerable trouble with the cushion tied round his waist! When it rained we had what is now called social dancing, and learned the Gay Gordons, the Polka and the St Bernard's Waltz. We enjoyed these lessons, but because I was fairly tall I had to dance the man's part which still leads to confusion to this day. To learn ballroom dances such as the cha cha and the quickstep, some of us went outside school time to lessons in the basement of the Gaumont cinema at the top of the Market Square. New dances like rock and roll were just coming into fashion; I have it recorded in my 1963 diary exactly when Miss Williams (later Mrs Allen), the then new games mistress, first did the twist. People now say that we must have had an exciting time growing up in the Swinging Sixties. In fact, most of the decade passed many of us by because there were hardly any opportunities to go out to dance. There were no discos; we had no television until I was seventeen, and so I did not often see dancing on the media. The annual Pytchley Pony Club party at New Year was about the only social event in my calendar, and it was a pretty staid affair. We were allowed one or two glasses of cider each. Under-age drinking was rare at that time; we had neither access to alcohol nor money to buy it. The only people we would see drunk in the street would be a few older men on a Friday afternoon or Christmas Eve.

❉ Ice skating in 1963 ❉

The winter of 1963 was a wonderful time for being young, but not so good for those who had to get to work or look after farm animals. The cold spell continued for many weeks until even the trees were creaking with their load of ice. Tobogganing and skating were plentiful in Abington Park and, best of all, the River Nene froze over in Becket's Park. Games lessons turned into ice skating sessions. A selection of ancient skates appeared from parents' attics and soon we were slipping, sliding or gliding on the white wastes. One High School pupil, Gillian Herbert, in the year above me, even got into the paper for rescuing a lady from the icy waters during one of these skating sessions. I do not remember any other year when we were able to skate.

Games lesson on the frozen Nene in 1963. Miss Rose in large furry hat!

Dressed for the weather in grandmother's skates.

❀ The ethos of the School ❀

The ethos of the school was very much set by the two headmistresses of my time. The first, Miss Marsden, in charge from 1937 to 1964, had established her strong personality long before I arrived. Her life and values would repay a study in themselves because she had progressive ideas for female education, expecting all girls to have a career of their own. Preparing for marriage and a family was not mentioned as an aim in life, unlike in many respectable girls' schools of the time. A devoted Christian, she stressed hard work in everything, hobby, sport or lessons, punctuality, service to others and particularly FINISHING WHAT YOU STARTED. She had a very striking international outlook and the first Prayers after the summer would be partly an account of her travels. One particularly vivid one described her visit to Russia, a rare event in those days of the Cold War. We were made very aware of the plight of the Hungarian people in 1956. Every Friday, Form Time would be extended for a session of Current Affairs where we were all supposed to bring a news item from the paper. At first *The Children's Newspaper* was handy for this but later it had

Miss Marsden (standing) at one of her last speech days. The Bishop of Peterborough is sitting second from her, next to the Mayor.

to be from a broadsheet. It was amazing what one could make up if desperate! Each morning Miss Marsden would park her small black car in Hazelwood Road. Any pupil who might be passing would be expected to 'volunteer' to help carry her piles of exercise books in through the front door and up to her room. The carrying was easy. At the same time, however, one was expected to discuss any issue of the day that was chosen that morning!

In one General Election, I think in 1964, we were encouraged to run a school campaign with the usual meetings, speeches, voting and sixth formers as candidates. Jane Collier won by a large majority. Not surprisingly, as the daughter of Alderman J.V.Collier who had had a long distinguished career in the politics of the town, she had run as a Conservative candidate with the slogan 'Be Jollier, Vote Collier' while another sixth-former, Jane Fowler, led a spirited Labour campaign. This was not representative of the politics of the whole town because it had long been a Labour stronghold, but it did reflect the backgrounds of the majority of pupils. We were expected to be informed on policies and to use our vote.

Miss Marsden, a rather unusual looking lady with somewhat shapeless

Miss Marsden's retirement dinner for governors and staff, past and present, in the Cripps Block dining room, 1964.

but quite formal dresses and iron-grey, fine hair that stuck up straight in all directions, had been head for twenty years by the time I entered Towerfield and in some ways had become quite arbitrary. She told a friend of mine later that if a teacher applied for a post at the school but her handwriting sloped backwards, the application form would be placed straight in the bin. She never changed. One old girl visited her shortly before her death when moving about had become difficult for her. The offer of a helping arm was politely but very firmly declined! On occasions when my mother needed to go to see her to discuss something, she tended to find the interview over and herself outside the door again without having broached the subject she had come for! Miss Marsden had developed some strange ideas. Whenever we sang 'Praise my soul the king of heaven', we were lectured on the need to hold the 'heav –' for three beats of music, not two. It was implied that it was a very common thing to do to hold it just for two beats. It took me some years to realise quite how peculiar this was. She always went everywhere at a kind of fast trot. She would almost run into Prayers each day with the head girl galloping along trying to keep up.

The short service did set the tone for the day. We sang a hymn from

Songs of Praise accompanied most days by a pupil on the piano. This could be nerve-racking for the pianist. I had tried accompanying once or twice in Towerfield but there was always the awful feeling that if I hesitated, the rest of the school would carry on without me and I would never catch up. Every Wednesday morning we would sing a prayer, either ' O holy Jesus, most merciful redeemer', or 'Now thank we all our God', or 'Lead me Lord'. These beautiful tunes and words have stayed with me to this day and each time I visit my mother in Chichester I look with affection at the new statue of St Richard with the words of his prayer 'O holy Jesus' inscribed on it. Miss Marsden raced through benedictions as if all the words were joined together, for example, 'Now-unto-him-who-is-able-to-keep-us-from-falling-...' It was many years before I could appreciate benedictions properly! End-of-term services were always particularly moving, especially in the summer when many of the Upper VIth girls were leaving. We sang 'O God our help in ages past' and listened to the head girl reading the passage from Philippians which starts 'Whatsoever things are true, Whatsoever things are honest...' Three times a year every girl in the school had to shake hands with Miss Marsden and say goodbye before leaving on the last day of term. Miss Marsden encouraged all things dramatic, as we shall see in a later section. She also encouraged public speaking. Each day in Prayers, notices would be presented by pupils. Games results, times of meetings, details of auditions would all be given by girls who sat at the bottom of the stage steps on the right and then climbed them to give the notice. We were expected to stand up straight and speak clearly to the back of the Hall, which was no mean feat.

I cannot write of Miss Marsden without mentioning Mrs Gee, a larger-than-life figure who helped run the school. I later discovered that she had been billeted on Miss Marsden when her school had been evacuated to Northampton and had stayed ever since. At the time none of us knew quite how she had come to be at our school. Her passion was Spanish, for she had lived in Argentina for some years, and the school had built up a fearsome reputation for Spanish by the mid-sixties. When we were in the lower school, the Upper Sixth formers were doing very well, winning various state scholarships and Oxbridge places and carrying off top prizes each year in the Hispanic Council oral exams. Older pupils found Mrs Gee an inspirational if demanding teacher, but in our eyes she was quite a strange figure, dressed in a purple Mexican blanket and often smoking Woodbine cigarettes in the nearby café as she taught the sixth form. There was something thought quite dangerous about her among our fairly conservative parents. Package tours to Spain were still a thing of the future. No one we

Miss Lightburne(on the left) at her first speech day, 1965.

knew had ever been there and so this devotion to all things Spanish seemed rather suspect to us and our parents. Miss Marsden and Mrs Gee were just coming to an end of their reign; I felt very much that a golden age would probably never come again. It was something quite remote from many of us, unless, of course, we did Spanish. There was quite an elitist feel about it. The only real literary study, for example, was to be found in the Reading Society run by Mrs Gee, for which auditions were held.

Miss Lightburne came in autumn 1964; fortunately for me as a classicist, she rescued me from having to do Spanish. Having done two years of Greek already, I wanted to take A level but had been told to take Spanish instead. Miss Lightburne, a much more practical, down-to-earth individual, had a hard act to follow after these two unusual characters who had attracted quite a devoted following. She soon stamped her personality on the school, however, and went on to have a long and successful time in charge. Sometimes I had to read Greek texts with her on my own in her room, the 'holy of holies', which probably did wonders for my Sophocles translations but was quite nerve-racking at the time. She certainly expected brisk translation and was quick to point out if I said something more idiotic than usual. A devoted Christian like her predecessor, Miss Lightburne offered more equal opportunities to all pupils. Still a woman of spirit, she recently travelled over Northampton in a hot air balloon to celebrate her seventy-fifth birthday. Her great energy and enterprise remain unabated!

❈ Annual events ❈

Four important events stood out each year, all concerned with music or drama. Each required a great deal of rehearsal time. The Verse Speaking Competition involved individuals learning and performing set poems. Two of the other events involved whole forms performing a song and coercing anyone who played an instrument to perform as well. Conducting the choir of one's own form could be hair-raising. I once turned round to face the audience, the adjudicator and Miss Marsden to announce that we would be singing 'Fairest Isle' by 'Pur-CELL', with the emphasis on the last syllable. Up jumped Miss M, quick as a flash, and yelled 'PURC-ell'. I then had to turn round back to the choir who were fairly incapacitated by this time, having had the name of a well-known washing powder shouted out! The competition certainly widened our horizons; I remember an older girl singing Handel's 'Where'er You Walk' very beautifully. But looking back, I feel the music education was rather limited; there was no school orchestra, for example. I certainly enjoyed class singing of traditional folk songs such as 'Down by the Sally Gardens' and 'Westering Home' out of the *Sing Care Away* song books, and I took piano lessons out of school, but most of my musical education came from listening to 'Your Hundred Best Tunes' on the radio on a Sunday evening.

The drama competition took even more rehearsal time, often at lunch times but occasionally after school, because we had to learn and act a whole scene of a play, usually by Shakespeare. Looking back, I find it hard to see how we managed, but we did, from the Lower III up, playing male roles and famous passages with great aplomb. It was certainly good practice for the school plays and for the steady stream of girls who went on to Drama College.

At the start of the summer term, we auditioned for the school play. Standards

The author as lowly scribe in The Merchant of Venice, *1965.*

were consistently high. I remember a wonderful production of *A Midsummer Night's Dream*, a *Merchant of Venice* in which I played a lowly clerk to Jane Green's Portia and Sheridan's *The Critic* in which Margaret Niven played an extremely funny Mr Puff. I have been surprised not to have seen her acting in the media, such were her talents at comedy. The greatest experience was a performance of *Dido and Aeneas*, an operetta by Purcell. Anyone who was in that production can still sing the words to this day. Mrs Nichol, the very gifted speech teacher (there was no taught drama in the curriculum), produced all these plays with flair and professionalism.

Once a year the Hall would be blacked out, a huge screen erected and for the whole afternoon a classic old film would be shown by a travelling company. The two I remember best were a very old version of 'A Christmas Carol' and one about life on the Aran Islands off Ireland. We would come out blinking into the afternoon light after a magical experience. Visits to the cinema were rare in our family at that time. I had seen 'Genevieve' and Cliff Richard's 'Summer Holiday' and that was about all.

Apart from these four events connected to the arts, during the early sixties the annual Toy Service was supplemented by gifts of food which were then distributed to those older residents of Northampton who were on a list supplied by the Mayor. In the last week of term we would go out in pairs, once we were in Upper V, to give them out. It was on one of these visits that we saw a house in the process of catching fire. We were up in the Barrack Road area and flames suddenly began to shoot from a bedroom window. We made sure that someone had phoned the fire brigade – from a phone box since mobiles were still unheard of – but then left it to neighbours. It was quite a shocking experience.

❀ Going home ❀

Going home for most of the school meant the short walk to the bus station and catching a bus to various parts of the county. For me it involved walking from school along Derngate to Mercer's Row in the town centre. After crossing Albion Place, the first hazard was the entrance to the bus station. Double and single deckers seemed to swing into the entrance with alarming speed; after the windows of the bus station café there came, even more hazardously, the exit. There was less visibility here but the buses were not quite so fast. After the bus booking office I would come to Mr Robertson's sweet shop. One old penny (0.4p) went a very long way - you could buy eight chews for that or four for a halfpenny (0.2p). A threepenny bit (1.2p) bought a large bar of toffee and sixpence an enormous bar of nougat. Next on the left was the rather gloomy, damp florist and garden shop called Harry Bowler before Swan Lane came up past the back of the Repertory Theatre. On a good day I might see the week's stars coming back from long coffee sessions in the bus station café. Many famous personalities started their careers at our Rep. Lionel Blair, for example, played the pantomime dame there five decades ago and could be seen round and about the area. When I went through a phase of wanting to act, I had no illusions that most of the actor's life was killing time in quite grim surroundings.

Then I would cross Guildhall Road; on the far corner, immediately opposite the Guildhall itself, was my friend, Ruth Lawes' father's shop, selling bicycles. From there it was along to the zebra crossing, across the island in Wood Hill with All Saints Church on it and then across to the bus stops. We were fortunate in Park Avenue North as the numbers 1, 2, 8, 14 and 21 buses all went very nearby. After we moved to Weston Favell it was only the number 1;usually however, I could leave school at 12.40 and catch the 12.45 Wellingborough bus from the bus station. I could be back to school by 1.50. We used excellent bus services. I took going through the town for granted. County pupils who stayed for school lunch had to queue up to ask permission to go into town at lunchtime. There had to be an excellent reason for going; the public library was on the approved list, and so many girls developed urgent needs to do further reading at lunchtime! At one stage Boots was put out of bounds and at another, Adnitts, our one department store in The Drapery. The reason for this was never stated, but everyone knew that a High School pupil must have been in trouble.

❀ Keeping fit and healthy ❀

There is widespread concern today about how unfit children are becoming. I would say that the Derngate pupils had to be extremely fit. If I think about running at break down from the top attics to the underground cloakrooms, up the slope and then down to the fence at Victoria Promenade to watch the Cooperative Milk delivery horses trotting downhill very fast as they made for home and their stables, or of going from a biology lesson in Albion Place through the main building (down then up, of course, not through the south door), out to Derngate and along to the very end and upstairs to Becket House, or of taking my freshly baked rock cakes which had found approval with the kindly Mrs Minty from the domestic science room in the Cripps Block up through the gardens, down through the cloakrooms and right up to the headmistress's room for her to have them for her tea, we were not only walking long distances every day but climbing many stairs, now regarded as one of the best ways to keep fit.

I do not remember much serious illness. Certainly people did get whooping cough, German measles, mumps and, very occasionally, measles but that would mean two or three weeks off school. Chesty colds could turn feverish; antibiotics were not in general use. We often felt very ill for four or five days, then really, really weak for another four or five days as we went through the convalescent routine of doing more each day and then rather shakily returned to school. This took more time and could be inconvenient for parents, although hardly any mothers did paid work at this time. I think this longer process may have led to healthier immune systems than the 'quick fix' use of antibiotics that we have today. There was one huge bonus of being ill. We were allowed a coal fire in our bedroom. The wonderful glow of the dying embers cheered even the sickest patient. Houses were not generally centrally heated; I remember my father would allow the small gas filled radiator to be lit in our hall only if the temperature dropped to below 40 degrees Fahrenheit! But we were generally healthy. I do not remember a single case of asthma or eczema in my class.

We also used buses, which environmentalists would have approved. A few fathers (including mine) who worked locally would drop daughters off at 8.50 a.m. but that was rare. Even then they often would not drop us at the school door. I would be dropped by St Giles Church and expected to walk for ten minutes or so 'to get air into my lungs'. (My father did very embarrassing things like going for an early morning run in Abington Park in the days long before that was a trendy thing to do. Occasionally I would go with him, dressed in my hockey kit; I still remember the bemused stares of the early morning bus passengers. On October 1st he would change to a weekly swim before returning to the morning runs in spring. He did physical exercises which he had learned in the Canadian Army in the Second World War. All this paid off. He was still able to beat his teenage grandson at tennis well into his seventies.) Second cars were almost unheard of; most fathers used the family car for their work and so they were not available either for school or for after-school activities. If a place could not be reached by bus, we simply did not go. There was no such thing as ' the school run'.

🎔 English, maths and science 🎔

The government at the moment puts a lot of emphasis on these three subjects and yet they have probably been the least influential in my life. In English we followed a fairly typical regime. In Springhill, we progressed from Janet and John books to a series of *Wide Range Readers* which contained a variety of stories and exercises, supplemented by *The Essential Spelling List*, which is still in print today. We bought our own text books at this stage: most would be passed on from daughters of friends. It was an exciting day when we visited Marks' bookshop in The Drapery or Slade's in Abington Street to buy a new one, as I did with one of the *Wide Range* series. I still have the two *Orpheus* poetry books. Epic poems seem to have been popular at that time. *The Lady of Shallot* and *Sohrab and Rustum* have never really excited me. Around the eleven plus time, my coaching consisted of working through *First Aid in English* which seemed to concentrate on learning proverbs such as 'A Rolling Stone…'. Most English by now was either 'Comprehension' (reading a passage and answering questions on it) or 'Composition'. Some titles of the latter seemed quite bizarre. I clearly remember, 'Write the story of your pen'! In Lower Third I greatly enjoyed *The Family From One End Street*, and this was the first time I collected a set of books myself, buying the other two in the series. Sadly I hear these books have been banned for political incorrectness. They gave me a great deal of pleasure. The most horrendous book we ever read was in L3N, *The Rose and the Ring* by William Thackeray. Looking at it now I am not surprised that as a nine-year-old I could not cope with it. Generally I would say we read some classic books too early. *Oliver Twist* did nothing at age thirteen to make me love Dickens. That has only come in the last ten years. *Jane Eyre* and Jane Austen's novels improve with age in the reader.

For O Level Language we had to do clause analysis, dividing sentences up into named sections, which I enjoyed because it seemed to follow rules. It stood me in good stead for Latin. Sadly there are few opportunities to study it at all now even though it gives the student an ability to use the language accurately. For O level Literature we studied *Henry V* and *Twelfth Night*, *Silas Marner* and *Lark Rise*, which I shall mention later. With the exception of one or two books, my English career was uneventful and rather tedious.

My mathematical career on the other hand was fairly disastrous. For some reason, although I was in P group, I landed up in the 'Maths for Scientists' section. How this happened I cannot imagine. I never understood maths at all. My poor mother tried so hard to illustrate fractions. I can hear her now: 'if you cut a cake into ten pieces and take away three of them...'. But it never made sense to me and I felt that two and two made four only because we all agreed they do. They could make thirty-six if we wanted them to! Before the O Level year I had to do the most extraordinary processes like differential calculus and I knew at the time that none of it would be of any use in my life. Fortunately in O Level year we had a very gentle teacher called Mrs Almond. Her joy when I occasionally got something right provided a spur to greater efforts and I gained a B Pass. (There was a scale of 5 pass grades and so a B was high.) My only conclusion was that as we were guinea pigs for a new syllabus they marked us all up because they felt sorry for us! I hardly deserved to pass at all.

In Springhill we did not know we were doing science, but what we did do was nature study. We were always encouraged to bring wild flowers and berries to decorate our form rooms (and once a year the whole school: this continued throughout the Main School). This was long before the days when picking wild flowers became illegal. I still evaluate autumn displays of hips and haws to see what they would look like in the form room. We had nature tables with birds' nests found in old trees, pussy willow buds in spring and so on. We were encouraged to use books; Enid Blyton's *Book of the Year* and *Nature Lover's Book of the Year* contained much information on fauna and flora. We borrowed others, like *Brendan Chase* by 'BB', from the town library. Paperbacks for children were only just coming in and so a book like Enid Blyton's would have been relatively very expensive.

By Towerfield I know we had started biology because I still have the examination papers, and I continued this subject to O Level. The first full-time male teacher, Mr Powell, came in 1961 to teach biology and we gave the poor man a hard time of it, especially over topics like the reproductive system of the rabbit! We did not dissect anything but the teachers had to. One day a girl brought in a dead lamb from her farm and he dissected that! A few of the class watched in fascination at the front. Others of us retreated in hysterics to the back and a few had passed out cold on the floor! At the back of the room was a large display of rather revolting objects: old stuffed reptiles and horrible-looking bits and pieces in pickling jars. Mr Powell seemed to major on 'The Digestion of a Ham Sandwich', but when I came to study anatomy and physiology a few years ago I could barely remember even that! Only that each part took a different route through the body! I did half a year of chemistry in Lower IV when I tried to grow a beautiful crystal without any success at all, and half a year of physics taught by a Canadian man who had just come from lumber jacking and had not yet, I felt, perfected his teaching techniques. I had several Saturday morning detentions from Mr Schwartz which, in my memory, seemed to consist of my un-knotting pieces of string for two hours!

Domestic science would probably count as science now. It certainly was very different from the home economics courses in local schools today in which students learn how to manage a home, complete with mortgage advice, consumers' rights legislation and so on. Talking about money would not have been thought a polite thing to do in those days. (I am not sure how we were meant to learn about it.) Part of the course was cookery, the idea being that if our mothers became ill one day, we would be able to save the family from starvation. We cooked rock cakes, Irish stew, ground rice pudding and other nourishing dishes. We also did theory: it never ceased to amaze me just how many properties one innocuous-looking white of egg could have!

In the sixth form non-scientists like myself had to take a period of General Science each week. This has been useful because exciting discoveries about DNA and RNA were being made and we learned a little about genetics. They also tried to teach us how to change a plug, with greater or lesser success. The assumption by then was that we would be working women and should be able to manage a house ourselves.

❀ Boys and Technology ❀

You cannot write about a school these days without discussing whether it is mixed or single-sex and how much technology it possesses. Well, the answer for the school in my day was we had very little of boys or technology. There were boys up to the age of eight in Springhill but they did not count! We girls all felt very superior in the first week when it was the boys who kept crying day after day while we confidently got on with our Janet and John readers or played in the shop. I was very fortunate to have an older brother with his circle of friends. With no playgroups or nurseries in those days, starting school could be acutely upsetting. When we were in Upper Vth there was some talk of holding a joint dance with the Grammar School boys; I am not sure this ever got off the ground and I certainly did not go. Very few of our class had boyfriends or if they did they did not talk about them; meeting boys was easier said than done! I do not think we suffered. It was strange to go to college and mix with men from other colleges, but somehow it felt natural. I had the advantage of an older brother, and so it might have been easier for me.

I have tried hard to think of any technology at school without much success. By the time we were in the sixth form there was one radio in the Hall. (I have read that the first school radio was bought by Miss Marsden very early in her time at the school), on which we listened to some brilliant musical appreciation lessons from the BBC Schools Service on Benjamin Britten's 'War Requiem' which I remember to this day. Also by the sixth form one television was bought for Room 10, but the only use for the set that I remember was for the first tennis six to watch Wimbledon! I do remember a cricket addict bringing in one of the new transistor radios that worked off batteries and listening to a test match during a maths lesson. One of the highlights at home was the Children's Hour serial at 5pm on the radio. The suspense created in its episodes was amazing and we found it hard to wait a whole week to hear what happened next. I became acquainted with many novels in this way, especially those of Noel Streatfeild, which I greatly enjoyed. Children's Favourites on Saturday morning was a regular fixture.

It is hard to believe now just how little technology there was. The only telephone that we saw was in the office. There were no mobile phones, computers, photocopiers, scanners or language laboratories. We did not suffer without the last of these. A very strong emphasis was put on oral work in both French and Spanish. I am convinced we spent the first year learning French sounds before we learned any French words at all! It was tedious at the time but it paid off; when we went to France later we were able to speak fluently. Sometimes we had French verse speaking competitions. I still remember much of Lamartine's poem 'Autrefois le rat de ville, Invita le rat des champs...'. Also we had to read out loud passages of French books we were reading such as Daudet's *Lettres de Mon Moulin*. By contrast at my husband's school in Nottingham they did more literary French than we did but had no idea how to pronounce it!

❀ Subject and career choices ❀

A lot of time is given in schools today to preparing pupils to make good subject choices at various stages and career choices later on. We never really had choices apart perhaps from whether to do Spanish or not because we were told which subjects we were going to take. There were four groups by Upper IVth: QL took three sciences and no history or geography; P could do history or geography, two languages and one science; Q took one language and one science and R concentrated on art, English and domestic science. This was actually quite prescriptive but worked out well for me.

When it came to public exams, we took the London Examination Board Ordinary (O) Levels in Upper Vth and Advanced (A) Levels in Upper VIth. Generally we took English Language O Level in Lower Vth. There was no notion of everyone needing five passes. An analysis of my Speech Day programmes shows that we took ones we were likely to pass, from one subject to seven. We did not take more than eight in the two sittings. Some boys' schools took ten but for us that was considered unnecessary.

Careers information consisted of a shelf of leaflets in Miss Willis's Sixth Form Room (and one had to be bold to go in there as she did not suffer fools gladly). There were various standard destinations. Certain training colleges such as Furzedown and Whitelands had a tradition of taking pupils from the school, as did certain London Secretarial Colleges such as St Godrics, and some universities; Westfield College of London University was popular for Spanish. Many of us put Nottingham on our list of six university choices because the Cripps family had given them a lot of money and so we felt an affinity. Generally there was quite a narrow range of options. Going straight into business was rare. My friend Rory McAra was quite trend-setting by going to work at Barclaycard, then opening up in Northampton. I remember several people going into occupational therapy, but not nursing.

❀ School trips ❀

School trips did not loom large in our life. In Lower Third we had made the visits to the museum, and once we walked down to St Peter's Church.

Chateau in the Haute Vienne where I spent some of my French exchange weeks. It was huge, but then, there were ten children and the maids!

Jumping Cigarette at the chateau – the best bit of the exchange. Hard hats were nowhere to be seen.

In the Main School, trips were confined to going to Wembley to see the England women's hockey team playing. With the emphasis on languages, many of us did a French exchange in the summer after Lower Vth, one year before the O Level exam. These exchanges could be quite gruesome because they lasted six weeks. I remember exactly what night mine started in 1963; my mother and I had travelled to London to stay the night near Victoria Station, ready to meet the French girl early next morning. We woke to hear the news that the Great Train Robbery had taken place in the night along the same track that we had passed over the day before! For three long weeks we tried to interest Martine, our visitor, in various activities and sites in our area and beyond. The only thing that ever brought her to life was a nightly game of table tennis!

Three weeks later I was on the Channel ferry with her. Her mother met us in Paris where we stayed in their apartment before going south to their chateau in the Haute Vienne to join the rest of the family of ten children! After that we went on to their second chateau in the Dordogne – all this in the days before French holidays were so popular here. I was not impressed by the drainage of the village in the Dordogne or the French way of driving on the roads; this visit ended my aspirations to study at the Sorbonne. The best aspect of the trip was the pony called Cigarette which I enjoyed riding. Looking back it seems inconceivable that 15-year-olds who had never been away before should have had to spend six continuous weeks with a stranger of the same age. A few exchanges succeeded and lasting friendships resulted. Many did not.

❀ Strange aspects ❀

One strange aspect of daily life was that we were never allowed to write on lined paper. From the first day exercise books always had plain paper in them. This may not have been cost-effective. I have maths exercise books from when I was ten and in long division I managed to get only one or two sums on the page! It was not until Lower Vth that I really began to write straight lines. I am not sure why lines were thought to be unnecessary.

Every first day of term we had to take a medical certificate and two shillings and ninepence (about thirteen pence). The medical certificate

A good illustration of the few prize winners at the front of the Hall on speech day. The rest of us were UNDERNEATH!

listed various dreadful diseases; our parents had to sign to say we had not had or been in contact with any in the holidays and say which we had had before. I had never met anyone who had actually had diphtheria until I met my husband. The money was divided between two and sixpence (12 1/2 p) 'entertainments' money (I presume to pay for the old films) and threepence (1.2p) for music for singing. It always seemed a strange amount to me.

One of the strangest events of the year came each Speech Day in the summer term. Since there was only room in the Hall for the prizewinners, their parents and the Governors, the rest of us had to sit downstairs in the Gym. The proceedings were, I think, relayed down to the Gym. But the bizarre thing was that when the time came we, the majority of the school, had to stand up and sing whatever the song was that year. But there was no sound relayed up to the Hall and so no one upstairs could hear us, which seemed a definite waste of time! I loved the songs – 'Fairest Isle', 'To Music', 'Creation's Hymn' – all wonderful to sing but maybe not in the Gym!

Some people have felt that having writing and speech lessons seemed strange. Since I had had them since the age of four, they felt normal to me.

We were taught the Marion Richardson style of handwriting. I was pleased to find it later in *The Puffin Book of Handwriting*. We had class speech lessons up to Lower Vth and I also took speech as an extra. Each week I would learn a poem and after a year or two, I started on the Guildhall examinations, transferring to the London Academy of Speech and Dramatic Art ones at the end. I loved these lessons and after I left school I - eventually - passed my teaching diploma.

There seemed to be a strange on-going obsession with CHANGING INTO INDOOR SHOES. I expect it was healthier for our feet to have variety, but it irritated me a great deal to have to part with my comfortable lace-up shoes for flimsier indoor ones with a button. I went to great lengths to avoid changing and used to keep two identical pairs, claiming, if challenged, that the two pairs looked the same. Then they could not prove I had not changed!

❆ Regrets ❆

One of the regrets I have is that I have gone through my life believing that I was hopeless at all things artistic. What, in fact, I was no good at was the weekly process in art. First we had to cover a sheet of paper with a colour wash (we were not allowed to leave a square inch of white). The powdered paint needed to be mixed with water and always seemed too runny or lumpy. We had to wait until the wash dried and only then were we allowed to draw on top of the colour. Somehow my sheet took most of the lesson to dry and I never got far with the drawing. From the pictures I still have I do not think that was any great loss, but I still nurture the hope that some day I will find something in art or craft that I CAN do. We never copied anything when drawing: it all had to be from our imagination. I feel sad that our art classes were so limited; art history was never mentioned, although we did have good reproductions of Picasso paintings around the school. It was probably because he was Spanish!

Another bigger regret is that we did no local history of the nineteenth and twentieth centuries. The development of the shoe factories and estates was thought in those days to be of no interest. By the mid-1970s, however, these periods were fully covered; there are now many books, such as *Life in*

Old Northampton, on sale covering the nineteenth and twentieth centuries. In the mid-sixties industrial archaeology was almost unknown, certainly in Northampton. Tom Osborne Robinson, the brilliant artistic director of the Repertory Theatre, was just beginning to lecture on the architecture of the shoe factories and the housing around them as I was leaving school. I still have a letter from him, written in his wonderfully artistic lettering from his house at 62 Derngate, about his coming to talk to the school in 1965.

A third regret is that I did not know any of the history of these school buildings when I was in them! Nowadays I feel more use would have been made of census records to find out who lived in the house. For instance in the Main School we could have known about the last rector's family and household which would have brought us even closer to the past of the building that we sensed all around us. For Towerfield, a wonderful leaflet came out in 1998 with brief details of the families who had lived there. How I wish I had known it at the time.

I have often regretted that I never studied Georgian England while at school. I covered the period up to 1702, but then there was a complete gap until 1870 which has not been good. In Towerfield we had a history textbook called *A Valley Grows Up*, which traced the story of one community through the different periods. It was no doubt a good concept, but sadly, each beginning of term, we seemed to start at the cave men again. I became quite expert on woolly mammoths, but their use in life is limited.

The other regret is that the school did not have a neighbourhood dimension. It was hard to make friendships with people out in the county. We all relied on buses and things were more formal in those days. It was often parents who would invite us to tea in the first instance and it was quite an occasion. Those of us who lived in Northampton did not necessarily form an easy friendship group.

❈ Links with the Bassett-Lowkes ❈

Derngate is now becoming better known because of Mackintosh House, number 78. W.J.Bassett-Lowke commissioned the work inside the house from Rennie Mackintosh in 1915 with the intention of it being completed by the time of his wedding in 1917. Mr Bassett-Lowke combined an interest in his father's engineering firm with design and architecture.In 1909 Bassett-Lowke Ltd was set up and became world-famous for precision engineering, especially of models, both industrial and for pleasure, and of miniature trains, both to ride in and to play with. The Bassett-Lowkes lived in the house from their marriage in 1917 until 1926, when they moved to another pioneering house, New Ways, which the German architect, Professor Peter Behrens of Vienna, had designed for them. This was on the Wellingborough Road, facing Abington Park. So the couple had moved from Derngate long before I went to the school. The world where I was more aware of them was that of church. Mrs Bassett-Lowke had been a Miss Jones of the long-standing Crocket and Jones high-class shoe company of Stimpson Avenue. All the family were members of Abington Avenue Congregational Church in which I was brought up. The Bassett-Lowkes were married in the church. Two of Mrs Bassett-Lowke's sisters and two of her sisters married two of the Allinson brothers, part of another shoe-owning family that also worshipped there. Two great-nieces on this side were at the school with me.

There were many manufacturers in the town from the Nonconformist or Free Churches – Congregational (now United Reformed), Baptist and Methodist. The High School for Girls, Church of England though it was, had long attracted their daughters. From the early days it had been stated that Nonconformist girls were welcome and would study the Acts of the Apostles when others were absorbing Church of England teaching. I had to struggle to be allowed to take the alternative for O Level Religious Knowledge – I nearly had to do the Church of England section, but I felt that was unfair as I knew none of the liturgy by heart! I really enjoyed the Ascension Day service each year with its predictable hymns and readings.

Mr Bassett-Lowke's family had had Congregationalists in it before. His grandmother attended Doddridge Chapel in Commercial Street. Interestingly, the minister of that chapel from 1829 to 1879, the Reverend Prust, had lived in Towerfield for many years in the nineteenth century. The Bassett-Lowkes were well known in the Abington Avenue church. I was five when Mr Bassett-Lowke died, but his memory lived on; his wife was very much around although she suffered from arthritis. The Reverend Owen Butler, his minister at the time, remembers Mr Bassett-Lowke walking (he did not own a car or a bicycle) up the Wellingborough Road to the church with Mr Herbert Glenn of Glenn's builders and he would sit very close in front of the pulpit. One lady remembers sitting behind him in the church regularly and that he was a great 'fidget', but everyone thought it must be because he had an invention forming in his head all the time!

I did not realise at the time but I benefited directly from many aspects of Mr Bassett-Lowke's work. As a town councillor for many years, he had been involved in choosing designs for new buildings, and, as Chairman of the Baths Committee, had been largely responsible for the new buildings on The Mounts which included the swimming baths where we swam each week. He had also played a crucial part in the foundation of the excellent Repertory Theatre in the town in 1926. The town's 'Theatre Royal and Opera House' in Guildhall Road had been purchased for the purpose but in the 1950s and 60s it was always known as 'The Rep'. Many

Pride and Prejudice, *Rep style, mid-60s. Ian Ogilvy as Mr Darcy with Beth Harries as Elizabeth Bennett.*

of us joined the Youth Theatre Group when it started in 1964, having been used to attending performances of the company frequently since we were quite young. The company remained largely the same for the season but the play changed each week: excellent productions designed by Osborne Robinson, for whom we felt an affinity as his sister taught at the school, delighted us with their range and variety. The theatre provided a wonderful resource for the whole area, one that we took for granted at the time. I remember a production of *Pride and Prejudice* with a Mr Darcy the equal of any on television.

I did not realise that I had other links with the Bassett-Lowkes. Apart from the two great-nieces of Mrs Bassett-Lowke, already mentioned, I was in the same form at school, and a close neighbour of, a great-niece of Mr Bassett-Lowke's. Until Janet Dicks published her book, I had no idea that her daughter Jane was so closely related to him. I often wonder what Mrs Bassett-Lowke thought of her two new houses. Was she excited to be part of a new movement? Northampton taste, not least that of those in the church, was quite conservative, and I wonder if there were a few eyebrows raised, especially over 78 Derngate? I wonder what her family thought when it came to tea?

❧ Did I work hard? ❧

Not really in the early years. At the end-of-term Prayers the grade of every single pupil was read out ranging from A+ to C-; term after term I was around a B and on my report were usually the words 'Eileen is not working to the standard of which she is capable'. However, I was always busy. In Springhill we were regularly planning concerts or sales to raise money for good causes such as Enid Blyton's Busy Bee Club. I cannot remember now what the ultimate destination of the money was. Maybe these were the forerunners of Blue Peter coffee mornings?

Some of us went after school to dancing lessons at the Phyllis James School of Dance at 81 Abington Street. (Little did we know we were in buildings next door to where our school had started.) At the age of six, I even danced with my teddy bear in the annual dancing display on the stage of the New Theatre in Abington Street. The theatre had declined since the heady days when Anna Pavlova and Gracie Fields had performed there. It closed in 1958, to be demolished in 1960. My dancing days were short-lived. I had repeated chest infections and our family doctor decreed that it could be a result of being at close quarters with other girls in a hot room before standing in the cold with my mother to catch the bus home. He suggested an outdoor exercise, and so I started riding, first at Pattishall with the Knox-Thompson sisters who later emigrated to New Zealand and then, at age eight, at East Haddon. Little did the doctor know how expensive the change would be. Riding clothes, lessons, horse box hire to shows all mounted up to some considerable sum.

We did read a great deal as well. One Saturday I was very unpopular at the town library in Abington Street as I borrowed three books in the morning, read them and returned them in the afternoon before the cardboard tickets could be transferred to the right tray. The books in the library all had dark hard serviceable bindings. There was still some suspicion of libraries because infectious diseases were thought to be passed on from the books. It was quite common to bake books in the oven if they were thought to be contaminated. I regularly also gave myself nightmares reading my brother's Famous Five books, often by torchlight under the bedclothes.

One school year when we were very busy apart from our work was IIc. Our young, enthusiastic teacher called Miss Cruxton seemed very exciting after the rather elderly Miss Phipps. We actually produced a lengthy form concert including a play written by Josephine Muldowney, called 'Professor Potts's April Ist' complete with a detailed programme, of which I still have a copy. Later, in Towerfield and the early Main School years, I was usually doing things connected with ponies and farming. It was long an ambition of mine to study at Moulton Agricultural College and maybe marry a rich farmer with many horses! Because we had no television, I think we had to keep busy and I certainly did my own projects on what I was interested in. Planning gymkhanas was a favourite activity. I well remember spending a lot of time doing this in Lower IV along with Jane Nelson and Beth Van Millingen who both lived in Ravensthorpe. The Pony Club gave many of us tests to prepare for. We were about equally divided between the Grafton Hunt branch and the Pytchley Hunt one. Saturdays would usually be spent either at East Haddon or helping a friend exercise her ponies. Many of us were in Brownies and Guides as well. I am grateful that I had time to develop my own interests and we never had to think about SATS or assessments. There were certainly no league tables to worry about.

When we went into Upper III we were joined by the girls who had come in on free places from the county. It was a real shock to find how hard some of them worked; many of them ended up in the QL group. They had obviously been well trained whereas our teaching, in maths for example, had been distinctly patchy.

Then, in Upper IV, things changed. During this difficult year I had a Mrs Hayes for French, a cheerful, encouraging and efficient teacher, a rare combination. Suddenly I wanted to work and made huge progress in French. It seemed to be a 'transferable skill' because in Lower V, I had the efficient, pleasant Miss Burt (later Mrs Moss), and my Latin improved beyond recognition. Third in the line of specially inspiring teachers was Miss Dimmock, later Mrs Willmer, who took us for Sixth Form history. Finally, Miss Alder came to the school for her first job as a classics teacher just as I started VI3. She proved a very good model of what a young classics teacher could be like and I was encouraged to follow this career path myself. I cannot explain the transformation in me over these years. My friends were a bit cross with me when I would not compare notes in tests any more, but something had changed which took me on to university and teacher training.

❋ Did the school prepare me for life? ❋

Yes, certainly, but not in the way often talked about these days - of getting a good job to earn a lot of money to achieve a high standard of living. That was not mentioned in the late sixties. Miss Marsden stressed the importance of hard work as an end in itself, with its own rewards of satisfaction. I think one of the underlying aims of a job, in Miss Marsden's view, was to make a difference in the world and to leave it a better place than we found it. I still find that a value worth cherishing and I have found the idea of giving being more important than getting leads more easily to lasting happiness.

The most important way school prepared me for life was not through the academic subjects but through the speech lessons. The poems I learned by heart each week, for example, 'The Humming Bird', 'Zebras', 'The Little Dancers', 'Haymaking', some of which I have always loved very deeply, have stood me in good stead at times when it really matters in life; before operations, for example, or in very long motorway traffic jams. All this has been quite expensive through the years! I now acknowledge that I am an addict of children's poetry books. I used to say I collected them because I might teach it one day, but now I know they are purely for my pleasure. For my birthday this year I held a poetry party where each guest brought a present of a favourite poem to read out loud. It was a good occasion where friendships deepened. That was a direct legacy of my time at school. I find it is quite rare to admit to reading poetry. Writing it seems to have more social acceptance, but that was something we hardly ever did and it was thought to be quite a strange thing to do! The poems, and also two books, *The Country Child*, which we read in LIIIT, and *Lark Rise to Candleford*, which we studied for O Level, are what have stood me in good stead for the rest of my life.

❄ **Postscript** ❄

By the 1980s, the school owned a substantial part of Derngate and seemed to be set to stay there. Alterations were made. Various gardens were turned into car parks and Numbers 54-64 were found to be unsafe and demolished. Then we heard that the school was moving to brand new premises in Hardingstone which would open in 1992. This was initially a shock, but eventually the Derngate site has been tastefully developed and, together with Springhill, has been rescued from a dreadful derelict period.

However, a world has gone for ever, and I hope this small book will help it not to be forgotten. I also hope that any of today's pupils who are interested will have the opportunity to read about earlier days at the school. There was a large living, playing, learning community in these buildings. Its members helped shape the future of many hundreds of Northamptonshire girls. Their legacy lives on and deserves to be acknowledged and recorded.

❈ Details of time at school ❈

Age	Form Teacher	Form	Room	Year
4-5	Miss Cook	Lower Kindergarten	Springhill	April-July 1953
5-6	Miss Welford Miss Cripps	Upper Kindergarten	Springhill	1953-54
6-7	Mrs Mossman	Transition	Springhill	1954-55
7-8	Miss Phipps	1Ph	Springhill	1955-56
8-9	Miss Cruxton	2C	Springhill	1956-57
9-10	Mrs Nichol	L3N	Towerfield	1957-58
10-11	Miss Thornton	L3T	Towerfield	1958-59
11-12	Miss Overton	U3O	Room 11	1959-60
12 -13	Miss Line (Mrs Beavis)	L4L	ChemLab	1960-61
13-14	Miss Jacques	U4J	Room 14	1961-62
14-15	Miss Clayton	L5C	Room 8	1962-63
15-16	Miss Morgan	U5M	Room 1	1963-64
16-17	Miss Emmett	VI 1	Room 10	1964-65
17-18	Miss Dimmock	VI 2	Room 7	1965-66
18	Miss Willis	VI 3	Room 8	1966-Dec. 1966

❄ **Bibliography** ❄

Janet Bassett-Lowke, *Wenman Joseph Bassett-Lowke* (Chester, 1999)

44 Derngate: The Inside Story ([Northampton],n.d.)

Judith Hodgkinson (comp.), *W. J. Bassett-Lowke: A Model World* (Northampton, 1999)

Life in Old Northampton (Northampton, 1976)

P.D.Nichol, *The First Hundred Years: A History of Northampton High School,* (Northampton, 1978)

Northampton: A Secret Past (Northampton, n.d.)

'Towerfield: 66 Derngate' ([Northampton], 1998)